From Cacao Bean to Chocolate

From Cacao Bean
to Chocolate

Ali Mitgutsch

 Carolrhoda Books, Inc., Minneapolis

First published in the United States of America 1981 by
Carolrhoda Books, Inc. All English language rights reserved.

Original edition © 1975 by Sellier Verlag GmbH, Eching bei München,
West Germany, under the title VOM KAKAO ZUR SCHOKOLADE.
Revised English text © 1981 by Carolrhoda Books, Inc.
Illustrations © 1975 by Sellier Verlag GmbH.

Manufactured in the United States of America

LIBRARY OF CONGRESS CATALOGING IN PUBLICATION DATA

Mitgutsch, Ali.
  From cacao bean to chocolate.

    (A Carolrhoda start to finish book)
    Edition for 1975 published under title: Vom Kakao
zur Schokolade.
    SUMMARY: Follows the cacao bean from the tropical
trees on which they grow to the factories where they
are roasted, skinned, and ground to make cocoa butter,
the major ingredient in chocolate products.

    1. Chocolate—Juvenile literature. 2. Cacao—Juvenile
literature. [1. Chocolate. 2. Cacao] I. Title.

TP640.M5713   1981   664'.5   80-29588
ISBN 0-87614-147-5

        2 3 4 5 6 7 8 9 10 86 85 84 83 82

From Cacao Bean to Chocolate

Wouldn't it be nice if chocolate grew on trees!
The most important ingredient in chocolate
does grow on trees: **cacao** (kuh-KOW) beans.
Cacao trees grow in places
where the weather is very hot.
They bear fruit all year long.

When cacao fruit is ripe,
workers use large knives to cut it off the trees.
The fruit is opened up, and the seeds are taken out.
These seeds are called cacao beans.
There are about 40 beans in each fruit.

The cacao beans are left in piles to dry.
Then they are put into large sacks.
There aren't many chocolate factories
in the countries where cacao trees grow.
So most of the beans are shipped to countries
where there are more chocolate factories.

When the beans arrive at a factory,
they are roasted in large ovens.
This brings out the flavor in the beans.
It also makes the hard skin around the beans
easier to take off.

The roasted cacao beans are put into a machine
that takes off the hard skins.
Then the machine grinds the beans.
When they are ground,
the beans turn into thick paste.
This paste is called **cocoa butter**.

The cocoa butter is now ready to be made into chocolate.
It is put into a huge mixer.
Other ingredients, such as sugar and milk, are added.
The chocolate will be mixed for several days.
The longer it is mixed, the better its flavor will be.

When the chocolate mixture is ready,
it is poured into molds.
It will harden in the molds
and become solid milk chocolate.
Then it is packaged and sent to stores.

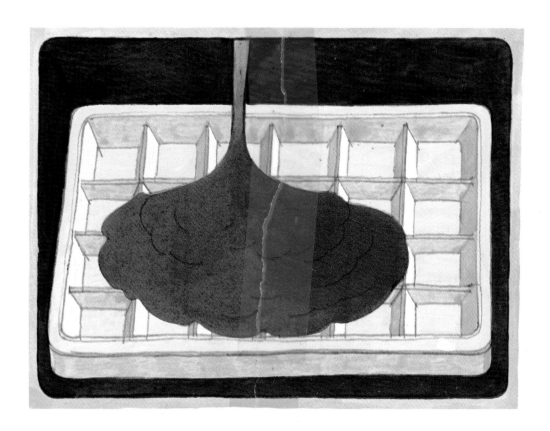

There are many different kinds of chocolate.

Milk chocolate contains a lot of milk and sugar.

It tastes very sweet.

Chocolate made with only a little milk and sugar

is slightly bitter.

It is often used for baking.

But no matter how sweet or bitter it is,

all chocolate starts with cacao beans.

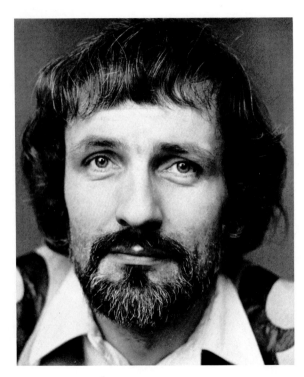

**Ali
Mitgutsch**

ALI MITGUTSCH is one of Germany's best-known children's book illustrators. He is a devoted world traveler, and many of his book ideas have taken shape during his travels. Perhaps this is why they have such international appeal. Mr. Mitgutsch's books have been published in 22 countries and are enjoyed by thousands of readers around the world.

Ali Mitgutsch lives with his wife and three children in Schwabing, the artists' quarter in Munich. The Mitgutsch family also enjoys spending time on their farm in the Bavarian countryside.

THE CAROLRHODA

START

From Beet to Sugar

From Blossom to Honey

From Cacao Bean to Chocolate

From Cement to Bridge

From Clay to Bricks

From Cotton to Pants

From Cow to Shoe

From Dinosaurs to Fossils

From Egg to Bird

From Egg to Butterfly

From Fruit to Jam

From Grain to Bread

From Grass to Butter

From Ice to Rain

From Milk to Ice Cream

From Oil to Gasoline

From Ore to Spoon

From Sand to Glass

From Seed to Pear

From Sheep to Scarf

From Tree to Table

TO FINISH BOOKS